Tackling *the* Troubles *that* Target Timothys!

Evangelist Justin Cooper
Forward by Dr. John N. Hamblin

Tackling *the* Troubles *that* Target Timothys!

Evangelist Justin Cooper
Forward by Dr. John N. Hamblin

All Scriptures are taken from the King James Bible.

ISBN# 978-1-61119-014-4

Printed in the United States of America.

Printed by Calvary Publishing
A Ministry of Parker Memorial Baptist Church
1902 East Cavanaugh Road
Lansing, Michigan 48910
www.CalvaryPublishing.org

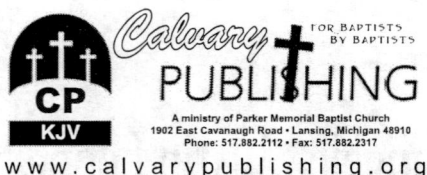

Calvary
PUBLISHING
FOR BAPTISTS
BY BAPTISTS
CP
KJV
A ministry of Parker Memorial Baptist Church
1902 East Cavanaugh Road • Lansing, Michigan 48910
Phone: 517.882.2112 • Fax: 517.882.2317
www.calvarypublishing.org

Contents

Forward by Dr. John N. Hamblin

I count it a wonderful privilege to pick up my pen and place my highest recommendation upon this profitable and pointed booklet, *Tackling the Troubles that Target Timothys!* by my dear friend and dedicated fellow evangelist, Justin Cooper. I have found these pages to be clear, convincing, captivating, concise, challenging, convicting, and completely scriptural. It is my prayer that this booklet will find its way into the hands of every young preacher who desires to be more than a "clergyman" but rather a considerable man of God!

Thank you Brother Cooper; for taking your call seriously and taking the time to write this tremendous booklet to touch your generation with the truth of total commitment to the ministry and militant fundamentalism.

— **Dr. John N. Hamblin, Evangelist**

The Purpose of this Booklet

The purpose of this booklet is to simply shine the Scriptural light on a few common obstacles that the starting preacher often has trouble overcoming. In no way do I claim to be an expert nor do I pretend to be overly experienced. I myself, at the time of this writing am 26 years of age. I have been in full-time evangelism for four years. The Lord has greatly blessed our ministry from the outset with a full itinerary of meetings, a weekly, world-wide radio broadcast, and the opportunity to share the platform as well as personal fellowship with what I consider some of the great fundamental preachers of our day. I have traveled across the country, from state to state, and from town to town preaching the Word of God behind pulpits in fundamental churches, conferences, and schools.

This is not designed to be a lengthy, scholarly discourse on the subject, but rather a short, general dissertation. My heart's desire is to share with (or "commit" to) preachers of my generation as well as those to follow some of the struggles, snares, and slip ups that often target and takedown "Timothys."

It is my prayer that God will speak to your heart personally and powerfully through this booklet. I am trusting and believing that the Lord will bring up another generation of spirit-filled men of God to faithfully ring the bell and raise the banner high.

— **Evangelist Justin Cooper**

Tackling the Troubles that Target Timothys

"And the things that thou hast heard of me among many witnesses, the same commit thou to faithful men, who shall be able to teach others also."

— **2 Timothy 2:2**

In an America that is analogous to a Jericho with no Joshuas, or a Mount Carmel with no Elijahs, or a Babylon with no Daniels, now more than ever men who have been called of God need to step up and swing the Sword! It's time to remove the spiritual training wheels, pull of the spiritual water-wings, say goodbye to the spiritual farm league and find your spot on the frontline of the Lord's work.

Fundamentalism has been blessed, saturated, filled with figures of the past that were giants for God! I think of the Billy Sundays, the J. Frank Norris's, the John R. Rices, the Robersons, the Roloffs, the Spurgeons, the Sightlers, the Oliver B. Greenes, the Moodys, the Malones, the Bob Jones Sr.'s, the Hyles's, the Hutsons, the Maze Jacksons, the (you fill in your favorites); that helped shape our movement, stir our world, secure souls, and stand for truth and right. Our past is rich and today, among our present ranks we have men of God doing great things and seeing blessed results. But while our parentage is worthy of praise and our present is pressing toward the prize it is the prospective, or the future of fundamentalism that I want to pinpoint through this booklet.

If fundamentalism is to continue, Timothys must step up! If the Bible is to be heralded and heard in future generations, Timothys must not stumble! If souls are going to continue to be won to the Saviour, Timothys must stay faithful! Until the trumpet sounds, the dead in Christ soar, and Christians are summoned to the sky the work of God must go on! It is entirely essential that the Timothy of today, the young preacher, the man of God who's just picking up the plow and adorning the mantle be primed and prepared to receive and run with the baton that is to be passed to them.

Timothy was Paul's protégé in the ministry. He was the Apostle's understudy. Paul was Timothy's mentor. Throughout the two epistles that bare the younger preacher's name we find inspired instruction that without a doubt profits all believers, but I believe serve as an added benefit to those just getting their feet wet in the work of the Lord. From the commencing of 1 Timothy to the closing of 2 Timothy Paul's pen provides Timothy with several significant subjects. We view verses that cover everything from modest clothing to a minister's conduct, from the marks of a Christian to the malignancy of compromise. The Apostle Paul understood the often obstacles and plenteous problems that a preacher contacts on a daily basis and offers Timothy pointers and principles that both examine and give insight on how to defeat these deterrents. It's here in the content of this pair of inspired epistles that we will come to, consider, and prayerfully, tackle some common troubles that target Timothys.

Youth

"Let no man despise thy youth; but be thou an example of the believers, in word, in conversation, in charity, in spirit, in faith, in purity."
— **1 Timothy 4:12**

Possibly the most common trouble that targets Timothys is the stigma of their age. Phrases such as "preacher boy" are often tagged and pinned to the man of God who is just stepping out of the gate. With this label usually comes a significant loss of productivity in one's preaching. In 1 Timothy 4:12 Paul is admonishing Timothy to carry and conduct himself in such a manner that his age would be eclipsed by his example.

It's entirely essential that as a young preacher one doesn't come off as immature and inexperienced. I cannot count the number of times I've seen younger preachers

> People need to feel and know that they are hearing from a man of God not a "Johnny-come-lately"!

who by their pulpit mannerisms, their use of certain words or phrases, or by their actions prior to stepping onto the platform, totally drain the influence and impact from their message and their ministry.

People need to feel and know that they are hearing from a man of God not a "Johnny-come-lately"! Naturally some of this will happen due to the fact that a young preacher lacks the pulpit time, as well as life experience of an older preacher. However, much of the bad light that is cast by being a "preacher boy" can be overshadowed by the conduct, conversation, and character of the Timothy.

It's important to take note, that in no way should a starting preacher ever suppose themselves to be in any way, shape or form superior to a seasoned preacher. The Bible calls upon all Christians to respect and honor their elders and this is especially important in the area of addressing seasoned men of God! Arrogance will move a preacher from the ministry's batter's box to the back end of the bench in a moment!

> "Rebuke not an elder, but intreat *him* as a father; *and* the younger men as brethren;"
> —1 Timothy 5:1

> "Let the elders that rule well be counted worthy of double honour, especially they who labour in the word and doctrine."
> — 1 Timothy 5:17

Today, at this point in my own ministry I am almost always younger than the pastor that I am preaching for. Often times I am asked for council or input from those with more years of preaching than I have living and who may be dealing with problems and situations that possibly I have not yet encountered. At the time of this writing I am many times half the age of the host pastor as well as most of his people, but I have encountered no resistance to my messages or my ministry. If a Timothy is going to succeed in their service they must tackle the trouble of their youth! I truly believe that regardless of one's tenure on the planet, they can still see great results from their time in the pulpit if only they will commit a few simple, Scriptural principles to their character!

Scriptural Astuteness

> "Study to shew thyself approved unto God, a workman that needeth not to be ashamed, rightly dividing the word of truth."
>
> **— 2 Timothy 2:15**

A sure way to stifle the stigma of youth is to saturate yourself with the Scriptures! President Theodore Roosevelt claimed, *"A thorough knowledge of the Bible is worth more than a college education."* Time in the study will add spiritual years to one's ministry! There is simply no substitute for a thorough knowledge of God's Word. The Bible commands all Christians in Colossians 3:16 to,

> "Let the word of Christ dwell in you richly in all wisdom; teaching and admonishing one another in psalms and hymns and spiritual songs, singing with grace in your hearts to the Lord."

The word "richly" found in this verse carries with it the thought and truth that the Bible should be in abundance in our lives.

Dr. Harry Ironside, commenting on Colossians 3:16, made notice of the effects of being "filled" with the word of God as stated in the verse. He then made comparison to the effects of being filled with the Holy Spirit found in Ephesians 5. Dr. Ironside penned, *"There is an old rule in mathematics that 'things equal to the same thing are equal to one another." If to be filled with the Word is equal in result to being filled with the Spirit, then it should be clear that the Word-filled Christian is the Spirit-filled Christian!"*

The Timothy must preach messages that do not sound like a children's church object lesson or a women's missionary society devotional. Burn the stool, give the journal back to junior and with a preaching voice thunder the Scriptures! Deliver substance with a shout and content with combustion! "Preacher boy" sermons always prolong the "preacher boy" stigma. One of the greatest compliments I have received was offered during my first year of evangelism. I had only been surrendered to preach a short time and was just beginning to hold my first few revival meetings. An older gentleman in the mountains of North Carolina said, *"You preach like an old-timer, not like a whipper-snapper!"* That off-the-cuff statement, though definitely not overly dynamic or deep was a great encouragement to me as I began in ministry.

Timothy, fill your mind with the Word, stuff your heart with the Bible then go and attack the pulpit like Beelzebub is backstroking in the baptistery! Study to shew thyself approved unto God (and it will go far with man as well)! This might require turning off the television, putting down the video game, skipping the afternoon nap, getting up early and staying up late. Don't sacrifice your time in the Scriptures; there is no substitute. The Bible must become a priority in the life of a young preacher. Do as one has stated, *"Study yourself full, think yourself straight, pray yourself hot, and let yourself go."*

Billy Sunday thought much of the Bible and saw blessed results in his meetings. He used to describe his experience in the Word of God as follows:

"Years ago, with the Holy Spirit for my guide, I entered this wonderful temple that we call Christianity. I entered through the portico of Genesis and walked

down through the Old Testament's art gallery, where I saw the portraits of Joseph, Jacob, Daniel, Moses, Isaiah, Solomon and David hanging on the wall; I entered the music room of

> Burn the stool, give the journal back to junior and with a preaching voice thunder the Scriptures!

the Psalms and the Spirit of God struck the keyboard of my nature until it seemed to me that every reed and pipe in God's great organ of nature responded to the harp of David, and the charm of King Solomon in his moods. I walked into the business house of Proverbs. I walked into the observatory of the prophets and there saw photographs of various sizes, some pointing to far-off stars or events--all concentrated upon one great Star which was to rise as an atonement for sin. Then I went into the audience room of the King of Kings, and got a vision from four different points--from Matthew, Mark, Luke and John. I went into the correspondence room, and saw Peter, James, Paul and Jude, penning their epistles to the world. I went into the Acts of the Apostles and saw the Holy Spirit forming the Holy Church, and then I walked into the throne room of Revelation and caught a glimpse of the King sitting on his throne in all his glory, and I cried: 'All hail the power of Jesus' name, let angels prostrate fall; Bring forth the royal diadem and crown Him Lord of all!' In teaching me the way of life, the Bible has taught me the way to live, it taught me *how to die."*

The Bible is not the preacher's rabbit foot, nor is it an accessory that pulls together a paisley tie and a pressed suit. It should be to the preacher what the sword is to the soldier, what the hammer is to the blacksmith; absolutely essential to their work. Bible study should be done earnestly, extensively, and expectantly if it is to be effective. The great preacher of yesteryear, B.R. Lakin would commonly call on preachers to, *"Waller in the Word!"*

Knowing the Word of God will add confidence and detract contrariness in the pulpit. It will increase your ability to give sound advice. It will enable you to convince the "gainsayers." Allow the Bible to make its way from your hand, to your head, and into your heart! Using Bible terminology and not the newest worldly lingo or secular slang in your sermons will lead those in the pews to perceive the younger preacher as, he should in fact be, a man of God.

A Sunday-schooler once mistakenly reported to his friend that they were having a great "re-bible" at their church. He meant to say revival, but what a great truth! It's the Bible that we need, the Bible that gets the job done, and the Bible that Timothys must peruse, practice, and preach. Routinely "re-Bible!" Be astute in the Scriptures!

Sharp Attire

"And having food and raiment let us be therewith content."

— **1 Timothy 6:8**

Paul is addressing an attitude that should accentuate every believer. We should be content with the Lord's provision. He explains to Timothy that if a man has food for his belly and clothes for his back he should be content. This is a tremendous truth. It is important for Christians to be content, but for the purpose of our study I want to pull the word raiment out from this phrase. For the man of God it's not just being content with the clothes you posses, but when we think of raiment in respect to a man of God it is possessing and putting on the right kind of clothes that is paramount. Like the priests of the Old Testament, the preachers of today should be distinguished in their duds!

"And thou shalt make holy garments for Aaron thy brother for glory and for beauty."

— **Exodus 28:2**

I'll never forget during my time in college I enrolled in a course covering the topic of classroom management for future teachers. The professor

> No one should have to guess who the preacher for the service is when you step into the sanctuary!

made a statement that has stuck in my heart from then until now. He stated, *"Apparel can either exude authority or it will exclude authority. It will either generate respect or it will cause you to give up respect."* How true that statement is! I cannot count the number of times I have been to revival meetings, conferences, or fellowship meetings and been introduced to young preachers who were wearing clothes that belonged in a school desk, not behind the sacred desk. When an athlete takes the field, they adorn a uniform. When a lawyer goes to court, they dress accordingly. When a surgeon goes to operate, they put on the appropriate attire! No one ever asks a football player, *"What's with the helmet?"* No one ever petitions a surgeon, *"What's with the scrubs?"*, and so it should be with the man of God! No one should have to guess who the preacher for the service is when you step into the sanctuary! If you are to error, lean to the side of over-dressing and never under-dressing. I am not advocating that the young preacher go out and purchase clothes that his money can't buy! You don't have to buy the best to look your best. Just present yourself in a way that does justice to your calling. Nothing about the work of the Lord should ever be "coach," but rather always "first class"; especially the appearance of the man of God.

In a day where dressing down is on the ups and casual clothing has moved from the mall into the ministry, the starting preacher, the Timothy must make it a pointed practice to present themselves as a man of God! While others in your age bracket and at your experience level are sporting open collars, Bermuda shorts, and catchy Christian wristbands, it is imperative that you implement sharp, straight-laced, sophisticated attire in your ministry. Look like a preacher not a member of the youth group or campus crusade! Save your sweater for the slopes, your polo for the putting green, your shorts for sleeping, and forget the flip flops!

Dr. Tom Malone Sr. once said, *"The preacher should not look like the advance agent for the rag man!"* and to that we say "Amen." Button your suit jacket, knot your tie, shine your shoes, iron your slacks, shave your face, comb your short hair, and present your self as you are in truth, a message bearer on business for the Master! Be sharp!

Seasoned Associates

"Unto Timothy, *my* own son in the faith: Grace, mercy, *and* peace, from God our Father and Jesus Christ our Lord."

—1 Timothy 1:2

In this verse of Scripture it is made quite clear the relationship that existed between Timothy and Paul. They were friends, they were fellow laborers, and Paul even mentions their family ties in the faith. Timothy, though younger and at a different stage in ministry as that of Paul, still made Paul his pal and vies versa!

The Timothy of today should follow this example and find themselves a group of "Pauls" to glean from. Possibly the most productive way to overcome the hurdle of youth is to allow older preachers to influence and impact your life and operate from their example from the outset of your ministry. Dr. John R. Rice once penned the thought that every preacher should serve a spiritual "apprenticeship." As a young preacher it is paramount that you surround and side yourself with preachers who have been in the race and are running it right. Elisha had Elijah, the twelve had Jesus, Torrey had Moody, Sunday had Chapman, and Timothy had Paul! Every extensively used servant of God had or has the fingerprint and spiritual DNA of another, more experienced servant of God upon them.

> Things you'll glean at the table or in the car or on the phone simply by listening to a more seasoned man of God can prove more profitable than a library full of instructional books.

Recently I read

the account of a pastor who was relaying to his people an inspiring incident in the life of D.L. Moody. The pastor explained, *"Years ago in our town the great evangelist, D.L. Moody was holding revival services. Each evening the entire sanctuary was filled from front to back with people. Some were even standing outside looking and listening through windows and cracked openings. A certain young boy, intrigued by the famous evangelist, waited outside the church for the arrival of Mr. Moody. Shortly before the start of the service a buggy arrived carrying the evangelist and his associates. Upon seeing the boy Mr. Moody looked down to great him. The lad stuttered and said, 'I've been waiting to meet you sir. I wanted to be able to say I shook the hand of D.L. Moody.' In reply the preacher said, 'Son you've honored me. Say, do you have a seat for the service?' 'No, the place is filled,' was the boy's response. The evangelist then told the boy to grab his coattails and hang on tightly. Mr. Moody then proceeded to enter through a side door that led onto the platform. Walking in front of the large crowd the boy was nervous and shaken but calmed by the smile of the evangelist. Mr. Moody grabbed a chair reserved for him personally and told the boy that it was his seat for that night. The boy enjoyed the entirety of the service sitting on the platform behind Mr. Moody! Then the preacher tied up his thought by saying, "This story is significant to me. For this was that very church, that very platform, that very seat; and I am that young boy! I was led onto this platform and today I preach from this pulpit all because I followed Moody and clutched his coattails!"* Young preacher, Timothy; find a seasoned man of God, clutch his spiritual coattails and let him give to and guide your ministry. Dr. John N. Hamblin, a man of God who has impacted and influenced my own ministry, one I count as a mentor, and the penmen of this book-let's forward once stated to me, *"There's never been an Elisha that has stepped forward but what they first spent time in the shadows with an Elijah!"*

Timothy, keep in company with those who are seasoned soldiers in the battle and you'll soon learn how to successfully fight the fight! I owe much of how I conduct my ministry and carry myself to the influence of older preachers. The Lord blessed us from the beginning to befriend several seasoned men of God and by being in their presence I was able to pick up and put into practice many things that others may only learn after years of ministry. I've heard it said, *"God gave us two ears and one mouth because we are to listen twice as much as we speak."* That is a good thing for the Timothy to remember. Listen to the conversations of older preachers. Take mental notes when they discuss their past experiences. Observe how they handle situations and respond to certain questions. Watch their body language and reactions. Things you'll glean at the table or in the car or on the phone simply by listening to and lingering with a more seasoned man of God can prove more profitable than a library full of instructional books. Get a role model, a mentor, a Paul.

I am afraid that many young preachers of the present think themselves to be a bit bigger than they are, spiritually speaking. With a freshly bestowed degree, brand new suit, or a few well built sermon outlines under their belt, many young preachers may see the older generation of preachers as having nothing relevant to relay to them. This is the worst mistake any man of God can ever make! The exhortation and experiences of older generations are an undeniable yet sadly, frequently untapped asset to younger generations. No preacher or Christian for that matter is perfect. All of us have our flaws and failures, but sitting at the feet of a Paul will provide you with opportunity to adopt and apply several good attributes. To tackle the trouble of youth that plagues Timothys, partner up with and pal around with practiced and proven preachers. Keep seasoned associates!

For the Timothy to tackle the trouble of youth they must have a Scriptural astuteness, sharp attire, and seasoned associates!

YEARNING

"No man that warreth entangleth himself with the affairs of *this* life; that he may please him who hath chosen him to be a soldier."

— **2 Timothy 2:4**

Charles Spurgeon once penned concerning this particular passage, *"Soldiers must be free from other business, and it is well for ministers not to encumber themselves with any other pursuit, but give themselves wholly to their Master's work."*

In time of war the ranks of recruits are composed of citizens that come from all walks of life. There are doctors fighting

> Preachers frequently and frustratingly play the part of the proverbial fly captured in the web of a spider.

next to ditch diggers, artists serving next to athletes, and wealthy warring along side of the wanting. Though an army enlists soldiers of different occupational and social backgrounds when the time comes to march to war, the tongue suppressors stay behind, the paint brushes are not brought, sports are placed on the shelf and there remains only soldiers. A good soldier knows his primary focus is the orders of his commanding officer regarding the fight at hand and all other things no matter the place of importance they once held must fade into the secondary. Paul, paralleling Timothy to a soldier adjures him to act accordingly.

Following his campaign in the Pacific during World War 2, General Douglas MacArthur delivered a dynamic charge regarding the duty of a soldier. *"It doesn't matter how much you have, so long as you fight with what you have. It doesn't matter where you fight, so long as you fight. Because where you fight, the enemy has to fight too, and even though it splits your forces, it must split his force also. So fight, on whatever the scale, whenever and wherever you can. There is only one way to win victories. Attack, attack, attack!"* A soldier distracted by things differing from their duty would have a hard time living up to the General's description of a successful soldier.

For the Timothys of today the temptations are many and multiplied that the world, the flesh, and the Devil provide to pull you away from the will of God. The word "entangleth" in our text verse means to be entwined or wrapped up in. Preachers frequently and frustratingly play the part of the proverbial fly captured in the web of a spider. Each week it's not uncommon to hear news of a preacher who was at one time ringing the bell and raising the banner but who recently sheathed his sword and returned to the world. I've heard it said that most young men that go out to set the world on fire usually return home for more matches. There are many yearnings that the young preacher must deal with and defend against on a daily basis lest he become entangled and ineffective. Here are three common ones to consider:

Companionship

> "A bishop then must be blameless, the husband of one wife, vigilant, sober, of good behaviour, given to hospitality, apt to teach;"
>
> — **1 Timothy 3:2**

Timothy is delivered the description and demands of a man of God in 1 Timothy Chapter 3. Throughout this discourse Paul pens the principles and practices that every preacher must fit and follow. The charge from the Apostle is that the bishop, or pastor, or for that matter, the preacher must be the husband of one wife.

Dr. Curtis Hutson once said, *"Adam and Eve had an ideal marriage: he didn't have to hear about all the men she could have married; and she didn't have to hear about all the ways his mother would've cooked it!"*

In spite of the often jokes and countless cracks it is a wonderful thing to be married. To have communion with another person that surpasses that of previous relationships and friendships. To have someone to provide for as well as to depend upon, to raise a family for God's glory together. To find a wife is to find a good thing.

> "*Whoso* findeth a wife findeth a good *thing*, and ob- taineth favour of the LORD."
> — **Proverbs 18:22**

But for the Timothy, the young preacher, this desire to have a companion can lead to disaster! It is of utmost importance that the girl whose finger you place a ring upon is God's girl for your life and ministry. Being a preacher, a pastor, an evangelist, a missionary is quite different from holding a job in secular society. The burdens that you carry will become your wife's burdens. The schedule that you keep will become your wife's schedule. The storms that you weather your wife must weather with you. She must have a surrendered heart and will for the work that God has called you to. A companion can either be your best asset or your biggest agitation. One preacher said, *"My wife is an angel… she's always up in the air harping on something!"* The preacher's wife and how she carries and conducts herself will have as much influence and impact on the produc- tivity of the man of God's ministry as anything else.

Your choice of a companion must be made according to the will of God lest you be moved out of the will of God! I believe the Lord has the right help meet for every preacher. The Lord has blessed me with a wonderful wife. She supports me in the ministry, prays for me, accompanies me to many of my meetings, and at times provides special singing during my revival services. She makes it possible for me to keep preaching across the country; not to keep from preaching.

Some preachers never marry, others marry too often. Be sure that as a young preacher, God gets first say on your choice of companion. You've got one chance to get it right and until death do you part to live with your decision!

Cash

> "For the love of money is the root of all evil: which while some coveted after, they have erred from the faith, and pierced themselves through with many sorrows."
>
> **— 1 Timothy 6:10**

After a long day of work, a man went home to his wife and young daughter. *"Have you got a kiss for your Father?"* he asked. *"No"* answered his child. *"I'm ashamed of you!"* he joked. *"Your daddy worked hard all day to make money just for you and this is how you thank me. Come on, how about my kiss?"* Looking him right in the eye, she answered, *"How about my money?"*

Without even mentioning names no doubt the reading of this verse brings to your mind and memory names and faces of those who started faithful, fundamental and fruitful but ended up flip-flopping or falling out due to finances. Our world today is driven by dollars. One man stated, *"It's dangerous when your yearning capacity becomes greater than your earning capacity!"*

When I first entered the ministry on a full-time basis I left laying on my desk a contract to teach history courses in a local high school. The pay for the position started at over $30,000 a year plus full benefits to boot. I had been teaching in a different school previously and received good pay and benefits there as well.

> **The hungering for money that consumes many Christians has no doubt led to the spiritual starvation of multitudes of sinners!**

When the Lord began to move in my heart and without a doubt was leading me into evangelism it wasn't easy to say goodbye to my current paychecks or the prospect of a better paying job, but I knew God was directing my steps and I'm happy in his will!

Today as I travel across our country and speak with young preachers and young Christians for that matter, I have found a troubling trend. Rarely do I find a young Christian today that either has already or is willing to surrender to full-time Christian service. Many have good aspirations as far as secular jobs are concerned, but I fear many believers that God could do great things with miss the boat just to make a buck. The hungering for money that consumes many Christians has no doubt led to the spiritual starvation of multitudes of sinners!

I heard the story of a man named Ralph who had fallen into hard times. His bank account was depleted. A friend tried to admonish Ralph to work for a living. His friend said, *"Ralph, you have two hands, do something with them."* Ralph replied, *"I am. I'm wringing them both!"* It should never be the Christian who is wringing their hands over the prospect of insufficient provision. God always provides for his people!

Charles Spurgeon recounted a childhood memory of his grandfather's need of a new milk cow following the death of their previous cow. *"My grandmother asked, 'What will you do now?' My grandfather replied, 'I cannot tell what we shall do, but I know what God will do. God will provide for us. We must have milk for the children.' The next morning there came 20 pounds for him. He had never made application to the fund for the relief of ministers, but on that day there was*

5 pounds left when they had divided the money, and one said, 'There is poor Mr. Spurgeon down there in Essex; suppose we send it to him.' The chairman said, 'We had better make it 10 pounds, and I will give 5 pounds.' Another 5 pounds was offered by another member, if a matching amount could be raised to make it up to 20 pounds; which was done. They knew nothing about my grandfather's cow, but God did and there was the new cow for him."

For the Timothy, a truth that must be continually on your heart and in your head is that your reward in Heaven will far surpass any thing you might have attained on earth. For the faithful servant of God, on the streets of Glory, there will be no regrets, remorse, or reconsiderations about a life of service; it pays to serve God! Outside of the future and spiritual blessings of being used of God I'll testify and say that in our four years of traveling in evangelism my wife and I have never missed a meal, never lacked for nice clothing, never slept under a bridge, we have a nice home, drive a nice car, and are able to enjoy our life together. Our needs are met and more often than not, our wants are supplied! What you might seemingly give up for God will be replaced a million times over by God!

Don't let the world's financial fanaticism blur your focus. Young preacher, you don't need the newest stereo, television, rifle, wrist watch, or muscle car. Live within your means. Trust God, have faith in God, wait upon God, your needs will be met in every way! You're storing up treasures in Heaven! Don't cave in to the cash craze!

Comfort

> "Yea, and all that will live godly in Christ Jesus shall suffer persecution."
>
> **— 2 Timothy 3:12**

Throughout this second epistle to Timothy Paul utilizes such phrases as "endure hardness," "endure afflictions," and in our text verse, "suffer persecution." Paul portrays to young Timothy the truth that being in the ministry is not for the momma's boy! Paul new what it was to suffer and he reminds his understudy of his overwhelming opposition in verse 11 of this same chapter. Here Paul pens under inspiration of the Holy Spirit:

> "Persecutions, afflictions, which came unto me at Antioch, at Iconium, at Lystra; what persecutions I endured: but out of *them* all the Lord delivered me."

Today, in a world that clings to catch phrases such as, "that was easy," the results of this just relax and run away from struggles mentality has infiltrated and infected young preachers in the ministry. Being a preacher, called by God, is the best thing a man can be! Better than being president, better than being a physician, but it is not easy. There are burdens the man of God must bear that other Christians never tote. There are storms the preacher must venture through that never appear on other believers' radars, and battles that must be continually fought. Being in the ministry is like being in warfare. It is a constant contest between those who are lifting high the Blood stained banner and those who'd like to see it lowered. If one strives to live contrary to the world they should not expect to be congratulated by the world!

Vance Havner penned, *"Christian persecution is not trouble in general. Everybody has that. Christian persecution is trouble that you get into that you would not have gotten into if you had not been a Christian."*

Your family may question your calling. Your friends may forsake you. You may not live in the biggest house or have the finest amenities. People may shake their heads at your separated lifestyle. To follow Christ you must bear your cross. These things should not be seen as a burden but as a blessing!

> "And they departed from the presence of the council, rejoicing that they were counted worthy to suffer shame for his name."
>
> **— Acts 5:41**

Mark it down; when a man of God becomes consumed with a need for comfort that same man of God will someday, if not already be consumed by compromise! A truth I evidenced growing up in the hills of West Virginia is that choosing the path of least resistance creates crooked creeks; it will also create crooked Christians.

For the Timothy, the yearning and the temptation is always there to lay down the Bible and pick up a briefcase, to run from their calling and run to the cubicle. It would be easy at times to quit on Christ for comfort. Oh, but if only you turn your eyes upon Jesus and see His nail pierced hands! If you'll visualize the smiling faces of souls gathered around God's throne and returning prodigals embraced by family and friends all because you stayed on the firing line! If you'll feel the heat of hell burning beneath you and feel the breath of heaven blowing upon you! If you'll remember the moment you surrendered, the moment you yielded, the moment you said along side the prophet, "Here am I send me;" quitting will be canned, stopping with be snuffed out, and temporal comfort will pale in comparison with the joy of serving our eternal Christ!

The source of the preacher's comfort is penned and portrayed in the writing of the unknown poet:

Christ my Saviour, Christ my friend;
Christ my treasure without end:
Christ when waves of sorrow roll;
Christ, the comfort of my soul.

Endure afflictions, endure hardness, suffer persecution, stay in the fight, keep in the contest. Don't trade your spiritual work boots for secular bunny slippers! Resolve with the songwriter, *"The world behind me, the cross before me, no turning back,"* and let Christ, the cross, the cleared out tomb, and your future consolation be your comfort!

Never forget that a trouble that often targets the Timothy is a yearning; for companionship, cash, and comfort!

YOKES

"Having a form of godliness, but denying the power
thereof: from such turn away."

— **2 Timothy 3:5**

A third trouble that targets Timothys are yokes.
A yoke is a farm instrument used to group or pair
two animals together in order to accomplish a task.
The Bible, at various times uses the thought of a yoke
to illustrate inspired truths such as the relationship
of iniquity to the unbeliever, the relationship of religious traditions to believers, and the relationship of
believers to unbelievers. In the preceding verses of
2 Timothy Chapter 3, Paul gives his protégé a plain
list of some 19 personas that the young preacher
should avoid at all cost. The clear command of the
Apostle to Timothy was to "turn away" from those
individuals. In effect he is saying, *"Don't lock arms
with that bunch!"* The principle of avoiding unequal
yokes is set forth in 2 Corinthians 6:14:

"Be ye not unequally yoked together with believers: for what fellowship hath righteousness with
unrighteousness? and what communion hath light
with darkness?"

This should be practiced by every child of God but should be especially pertinent to the man of God.

I heard the story of a hunter and a hungry bear that seems to illustrate the often fate of those who yoke themselves to someone or something that is not in their best interest. *"A hunter raised his rifle and took careful aim at a large bear. When about to pull the trigger, the bear spoke in a soft soothing voice, 'Isn't it better to talk than to shoot? What do you want? Let's negotiate the matter.' Lowering his rifle, the hunter replied, 'I want a fur coat.' 'Good,' said the bear, 'that is a negotiable question. I only want a full stomach, so let us negotiate a compromise.' They sat down to negoti*ate and after a time the bear walked away alone. The negotiations had been successful. The bear had a full stomach, and the hunter had his fur coat!" That hunter could preach a powerful message on the dangers of yoking up with the wrong bunch! Be careful who you sit down with. Be careful who you negotiate with. Be careful who you deal with. Be careful of your yokes. Good yokes are always beneficial while bad yokes are always bankrupting!

As a young preacher the risks are high when it comes to fellowshipping, following, and falling in with the wrong crowd. The desire to fit in, the need of meetings, the want of fellowship, timely trends, the studying of materials that are not biblically positioned, lack of knowledge, wisdom, and experience all lend themselves to driving the Timothy into a detrimental yoke. I have found that if you will stay faithful, stay in the Bible, stay on track, that God will guide you to the right company. It is vital that as a young preacher, from the outset of your ministry, you take the right steps to starting and staying right!

Define Your Crowd

> "Do thy diligence to come before winter. Eubulus greeteth thee, and Pudens, and Linus, and Claudia, and all the brethren."
> — **2 Timothy 4:21**

I'd like to draw your attention to the phrase, "and all the brethren." In Paul's concluding comments to Timothy he sends the young preacher salutation from a specific crowd of believers. To Timothy these were common names and close friends. This was Timothy's crowd.

I remember as a teenager in the youth group how I hated the ice-breaking exercises that came with combined youth activities with other churches. We would have to do some kind of game or other activity at the start of the program that would require us to join with someone not from our church and whom we didn't know. This made me uncom-

fortable. I was hap-
py with the people
I knew. I was com-
fortable with them.
I was content with

> "I'd rather roam all of Texas alone than pitch camp with the wrong crowd!

my crowd. I am not preaching against such activities for youth programs at all, in fact, they are prob-
ably good and healthy to get young people out of
their "shell." I am just stating a point that even early
in life and in all areas of life people are prone to pick
a crowd and gravitate toward certain people to partner with!

I once heard famous radio personality, Paul
Harvey tell a story of an indecisive Civil War soldier. The man couldn't decide if he wanted to fight
for the North or if he would fight for the South. To
solve his problem the soldier decided to adorn a
blue jacket and at the same time wear grey pants.
He ventured cautiously onto the battlefield and was
shot from both directions!

For the Timothy of today to stay clear of detrimental yokes they must define their crowd from the
start. Now, be sure not to misinterpret the meaning
of this point. I am not advocating selling one's soul
to a man-centered camp. I believe it's safe to say that
I am in the Jesus crowd, the God crowd, the Bible
crowd, but at the same time let me add that not all
those who name the name of Christ are part of or

promoting the right crowd! Not every church is in the right crowd, not every Christian school is in the right crowd, and definitely not every denomination is in the right crowd. The best way, the only way to find your crowd and to be sure it is the right crowd is to choose your crowd based according to Bible truth. It must be the Word of God and not family ties, local customs, popular opinion, private interpretation, or retirement plans that place the preacher in his party! If at any point you see things in a denomination, school, or religious group that flows contrary to the current of Scripture you can unapologetically mark them as the "wrong crowd."

It's from using this method of measuring every mark of a group against the Bible's message that made me and keeps me an independent Baptist. I am not an independent Baptist for applause, convenience, or any other motive. I came to the conclusion, based on the Bible, that if I was going to be a Christian and be true to every bit of the Word of God, then without question I would be an independent, fundamental Baptist!

There are three things that should be a must for every Timothy when defining their crowd:

Authoritative Text

If a group doesn't have an authoritative manual they will always malfunction. A text that is not to be debated or divided, undermined or overshadowed. The King James Bible is the only Bible I use and endorse. I believe it is the inspired, preserved Word of God. Therefore, naturally "my" crowd (and payerfully yours as well) is the King James Bible crowd. An authoritative text!

Attitude of Triumph

A crowd that is always pouting and pouching their lips and talking about how hard it is and how bad it's getting is not the right crowd for a Timothy. Find a group that believes God is alive and well, still on the throne, still saving sinners, and still sending revival! This will do much to motivate your own ministry. A positive mindset will go a long way in producing a productive ministry. An attitude of triumph!

Astounding Track Record

A crowd that doesn't follow the Great Commission, doesn't see church growth, offers the sights and sounds of worldliness in their worship, and has a history of unbiblical hang-ups sounds better fitted for a toe-tag than a Timothy! Get in a group with a blessed history and a bright future. A soul-winning, separated, spirit-filled, Scriptural crowd. An astounding track record!

I once heard a statistic stated years ago that said,

"All the people in the world could live in Texas if they could only get along together." The person who stated that was putting across the idea that if we would just be friendly toward everyone then we could all live inside the perimeter of that state. I said that to simply say this, there is nothing wrong with being friendly. In fact, a fundamentalist that is not friendly shouldn't call themselves a fundamentalist! As Christians and as preachers we aren't called on to be crude, rude, and in a bad mood, but at the same time, when it comes to drawing lines of fellowship and determining the yokes that one is going to wear I have no reservations allowing the Bible to boundary and the Scriptures to separate! I'd rather roam all of Texas alone than pitch camp with the wrong crowd!

Billy Sunday thundered, *"You can't love flowers without hating weeds!"* It bothers me today to watch as men of God within my age bracket and even those without are rubbing elbows, easing in, and inviting the influence of those, who in years gone by a fundamentalist would have no dealings with, to take part and have place in their ministries! We should be daily pressing toward higher ground, not slipping back toward the barrel's bottom! The Charismatics aren't my crowd! The Calvinists aren't my crowd! The Contemporary churches aren't my crowd! The "come together as one" movement (never minding doctrinal differences and Bible principles) is not my crowd! And so on. Define your crowd!

Declare Your Convictions

> "Preach the word; be instant in season, out of season; reprove, rebuke, exhort with all longsuffering and doctrine."
>
> — **2 Timothy 4:2**

A sure way to avoid yokes that are not advantageous is to proclaim your stand every time you preach the Scriptures! At my ordination service I wrote down a number of things that were delivered unto me by the men of God that I knew would profit me not just for that moment but throughout the expanse of my entire ministry. Among those things I wrote down was this statement, *"Every time you stand to preach you should be giving your doctrinal statement."* I think that is an awesome and accurate assertion. If the Timothy, the young preacher proclaims his position when he preaches many of those who differ or are soft on fundamental issues will as a result shy away and steer clear. You should never preach to simply come off as confrontational though that may happen, but

> **If you have Bible for your position don't blush or back up at proclaiming it!**

you should be clear, concise, and conclusive! Every time you preach the Word declare your convictions. No one sitting in the pews should have to wonder where you stand by the time you step out of the pulpit. If you have Bible for your position don't blush or back up at the proclaiming it! Preach the word!

Just recently in a revival meeting a dear woman came to me before I preached and asked me what I thought of the Jehovah's Witnesses (falsely so-called). I told her that I believe they are a cult, misled by a man, and in need of the truths of the Word of God. This troubled her for a moment, but after sharing with her a few Bible passages and then paralleling them with what the "JW's" pilfer she began to realize there was a vast difference. I then proceeded later in the service to preach on hell as if I had felt the fire and she was about to! If I had kept my convictions silent and given space to her viewpoint then in reality I would have been lending my "ok" to such a thing. Instead I stuck by and stated my convictions and she was, to an extent, educated and enlightened. If you won't stand firm on your convictions when pressured by the "wrong crowd" then you will lose all influence and effectiveness that you might have possessed when preaching with and to the "right crowd"! Dr. Bob Jones, Sr. used to say, *"A man who has no enemies is no good. You can't move forward without producing friction."* Be bold with

Bible truth!

Growing up in the countryside of West Virginia it is almost a given that one will become a deer hunter. As a young person and to this day I take to the deer woods each fall searching for a "wall-hanger." The first thing I do when I enter the area that I'll be hunting is look for a sturdy tree to attach my treestand to and climb up for that day's hunt. There have been many times I've looked over trees and found that after close examination they were to flimsy, rotten or weak for me to climb on them and feel comfortable. I like to hunt, but I'm not willing to risk my life just to end Bambi's! I thought about my hunting experiences and this principle of "weak trees" and can't help but wonder how God feels about those preachers who are weak on convictions. I think it's safe to say that just as a hunter avoids getting on a weak tree, so God will avoid "getting on" a flimsy preacher that is weak on convictions!

My first year in evangelism I received phone calls and invitations from many different churches from varying denominations. Being the new guy I guess they supposed that I would be willing to join hands with anyone for a meeting. Already knowing in my heart that I would never preach in such a place as those, I would invite the pastor or people from that particular place to come hear me preach. If they could not come to hear me then I would send them a complimentary sermon CD. I discovered that after hearing me preach, whether in the sanctuary or on their stereo, those places and people that weren't traveling in my direction usually got the drift and I cordially declined. Since that time the phone calls from places like that have ceased, invitations from the right places have continued to increase! I have also since made it a point to place abbreviated doctrinal statements on my prayer cards and newsletters. Each item I mail out reads somewhere on it, *"Independent, Fundamental, KJV."* Simply stating your convictions, in your sermons, on your stationary, or on your website will help the Timothy avoid the wrong kind of yokes. Declare your Convictions!

Decisively Continue

"But continue thou in the things which thou hast learned and hast been assured of, knowing of whom thou hast learned *them;*"
— **2 Timothy 3:14**

As a Timothy, a young preacher, after you define your crowd and declare your convictions you must then decisively continue in that direction! Wavering, waffling, or becoming wish-washy in position will swerve a person off their present direction and steer them down a pathway to detrimental partnerships. Timothy is here charged by Paul to "continue", stay the same, to be concrete and consistent with the truths that he had been relayed and had received.

Growing up we would often play backyard football, baseball or basketball games in our neighborhood. Without exception there was always one kid, who during the course of the game would decide suddenly that he would rather be on the other team and cause a commotion. I could list those by name, but I'll spare them.

> " Now, not tomorrow, not in a number of years, but now is the right time for you, to make a covenant with your own heart that you, by the grace of God are going to stay true to truth!

They are still fresh in my memory as being turncoats, "Benedict Arnolds!" It's hard to get over someone switching sides without cause or claim.

Truth never changes with the currents of the time, rather truth creates the current and we are then under obligation to move complimentary with it! Churches change, schools change, preachers change, society will change, but the Bible stays the same! If it is right in light of the Bible today it is going to be correct tomorrow. Bible-based convictions, rooted and grounded in the soil of Scripture should never be pulled up or plucked out of our heart.

"...continue thou in the things which thou hast learned..."

Timothy of today; continue in soul-winning, continue in separation, continue with the inspired, preserved Scriptures, continue with the local, independent, sanctuary, continue in the blood of Christ, the virgin birth, the glorious resurrection, and the second coming! Continue! Don't give into pressure, don't cater to people, and don't sway with popular winds! Stay with what's right, stay with what works; stay with Bible truth. Continue!

When your friends forsake you, continue. When your family labels you, continue. When the world laughs at you, continue. When the local pastoral association slanders you, continue. When the once faithful servant falters, continue. When Satan devils you, continue. When souls are being won, continue. When homes are being strengthened, continue. When the church is growing, continue. When your calendar is full, continue. Sun or Storm, gloomy or good; just continue!

"Let us hold fast the profession of *our* faith without wavering; (for he *is* faithful that promised;)"
                                        — **Hebrews 10:23**

Jonathan Edwards, known for his sermon, *"Sinners in the Hands of An Angry God,"* and instrumental in the American Great Awakening recorded in his personal journal at age nineteen, *"Resolved that all men should live to the glory of God,"* Then he added, *"Resolved, second, that whether others do this or not, I will."* Jonathan Edwards was possessed by a great conviction. Many of those who find themselves hooked into the harness of an unhealthy yoke can trace their being so to a time in life where they became lax or loose on their position or on their stand. Now, not tomorrow, not in a number of years, but now is the right time for you, the young preacher, the Timothy to make a covenant with your own heart that you, by the grace of God are going to stay true to truth! Dr. Shelton Smith, president and editor of the Sword of the Lord, once proclaimed in my hearing, *"Hold on tight to God's truth!"* That charge should be the heart-cry of every man of God. Continue down the right road, the Bible road. Don't waver! Hold tight! Continue!

If the Timothy will define their crowd, declare their convictions, and decisively continue it will help them tackle the trouble of yokes!

A Charge In Conclusion

"This charge I commit unto thee, son Timothy, according to the prophecies which went before on thee, that thou by them mightest war a good warfare;"

— 1 Timothy 1:18

Today in an era of pessimistic preachers and contrary Christians the work of God and the world at large are both ripe and ready for a new generation of Timothys who believe and preach the Bible without apology. Great things for God can and are still being done. The Saviour is still risen, God remains on the throne and the Gospel still gets results. God still works through the man of God!

Youth, yearnings, and yokes are just three troubles that the Timothy must tackle. The temptations and troubles for the servant of God are in abundant array. In no way is this writing an exhaustive investigation of them all. Each day the preacher must be on guard, sober, vigilant, watching against the smallest pit fall, problem, or possibility that could cause him to strike out. By the

> Being a young preacher doesn't have to mean you must wade in the kiddy pool of Christian service while others dive into the deep end. God can use you now!

grace of God some Timothy who reads this booklet should resolve to be a preacher, a man of God that will equip and enable himself to be used to his utmost for God's glory.

Being a young preacher, a Timothy, does not have to mean you must wade in the kiddy pool of Christian service while others dive into the deep end. God can use you now! There are many things that the young preacher, or Timothy can do to make their ministry more effective. The truths and thoughts presented in this booklet are only a small measure of the vast and valuable things contained inside the covers of the Word of God.

It is my conviction, as well as my personal experience that applying the advice given in *"Tackling the Troubles that Target Timothys!"* will be a great help and asset to the young man of God. It is through this booklet that I am prayerfully committing things that I have "heard" to those who'll read this booklet's contents. Therefore, in closing, I charge thee with the following:

- The Timothy must live in and learn their Bible. Preach Bible messages!
- The Timothy must present himself in raiment that is reminiscent of a man of God.
- The Timothy should surround himself with more seasoned preachers and Christians to glean from.

- The Timothy should not be hurried in finding a companion, but rather allow God to guide him to the right girl.
- The Timothy should remember that our motive is not a salary but the Saviour, God's glory not greenbacks!
- The Timothy must be content to war a good warfare. To miss out on some of the things others may take comfort in. Those who choose comfort over consecration won't know the joy of conquering!
- The Timothy must define his crowd. Let the Bible define it for you. He must stand by and state firmly his convictions.
- The Timothy must stay in the race, continue, not looking for a parking place but reaching for the prospective prize! Seek the Spirit's fullness in your life. Be a soul winner. Live separated unto the Lord. Strive to fulfill your calling. Look unto Jesus!

"And the things that thou hast heard of me among many witnesses, the same commit thou to faithful men, who shall be able to teach others also."
    — 2 Timothy 2:2

If God has spoken to you through this booklet on any number of points, would you make yourself available to him? Pray and ask the Lord to use you, to keep you from these common troubles, and to be glorified through your life and ministry. If the Lord has led you to make a decision through the pages of this booklet, we ask that you take some time and drop us a note and let us join in prayer with you. There is no greater life than a life lived for Jesus and we would count it a blessing to assist you in any way!

To Contact or Correspond with Evangelist Cooper:

Evangelist Justin Cooper
285 Prospect Drive
Cottageville, WV 25239
Phone: 304-377-6400
Website: www.evangelistjustincooper.com